SMALL STEPS *for* BIG CHANGE

REWARD CHART
Sticker Book

I AM GRATEFUL

HEALTHY EATING

REDUCE! REUSE! RECYCLE!

FiVE M.LE

GRATITUDE

Stick your gratitude reward stickers below!

Well done on writing down so many
wonderful things you are grateful for!
You receive a special reward of:

....

Gratitude

It is important to remember what you are grateful for. This helps to create a happy, positive mindset.

Are you grateful for:

Your favourite meal?

A bright, sunny day?

A cuddle from your pet?

Your family and friends?

Write down three things you are grateful for:

1. _____

2. _____

3. _____

HEALTHY EATING

Stick your healthy eating reward stickers below!

HEALTHY EATING

Well done on eating so many healthy meals! You receive a special reward of:

HEALTHY EATING

Healthy Eating

Eating lots of healthy foods like fruits and vegetables keeps your tummy happy! Practise a balanced diet full of healthy oils, fats and protein.

Let's eat something healthy!

FRUITY FACES

Make eating fruit fun by creating 'fruity faces'! Have a grown-up cut up different pieces of fruit for the eyes, nose, mouth and hair.

SMOOTHIE GOODNESS

Find it hard to get your daily veg? Blend up your favourite veggies with some ice for a delicious smoothie!

Stick your reading reward stickers below!

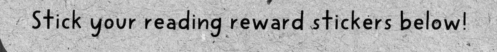

Well done on reading so many stories!
You receive a special reward of:

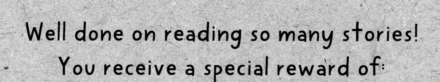

Reading a Book

Reading a book is one of the best ways to relax. Curl up in a comfy spot with your favourite book and get lost in your imagination!

REDUCE, REUSE, RECYCLE!

Stick your recycling reward stickers below!

Well done reducing your waste!
You receive a special reward of:

Reduce, Reuse, Recycle!

A great way to reduce your waste is to recycle! Have a grown-up help you to recycle some of your rubbish at home.

What can I recycle?

Glass bottles and jars

Metal cans

Paper, cartons and cardboard

Plastic bottles, tubs, jugs and jars

TIP: Make sure you wash out your glass or plastic before recycling!

COMPOSTING

Stick your composting reward stickers below!

Well done reducing your waste!
You receive a special reward of:

----

composting

Composting your leftover food means that nothing goes to waste!

WHAT CAN I COMPOST?

Fruit and vegetable scraps

Stale or mouldy bread

Coffee grounds and tea bags/leaves

Fresh grass, plants, stalks and flowers

A COMPOST BIN NEEDS:

A sunny but shady spot in the garden with good drainage

Lots of yummy leftovers

Layers of different waste materials

Air to keep the worms happy!

COMPOST

MINDFULNESS

Stick your mindful reward stickers below!

Well done on practising mindfulness!
You receive a special reward of:

Mindfulness

Learning to how to be mindful is very important. It helps you to be in the moment, manage your emotions and feel calmer during the day.

Here are some easy ways to practise mindfulness at home:

LISTEN TO YOUR BREATHING:

Sit down in a quiet place. Close your eyes and take a big, deep breath in for 4 seconds and out for 4 seconds. Repeat this for 2 minutes.

FOLLOW YOUR HEARTBEAT:

Dance around the room. Do big jumps, twists and turns!

Then, lie down on the floor. Close your eyes and place your hands over your chest to feel your heartbeat.

Focus on your heartbeat for a few minutes. Notice as your heartbeat goes from quick and fast to slow and steady.

FINDING IT HARD TO CONCENTRATE?

Imagine you're blowing up a bubble with your breath. Every time you breathe in, your bubble gets bigger. When you breathe out, the bubble floats away.

MOVING YOUR BODY

Stick your body-moving reward stickers below!

Well done on moving your body lots and lots! You receive a special reward of:

Moving Your Body

Your body loves to move! Make sure you move your body every day to keep it happy and healthy!

Here are some easy ways to move your body:

STAR JUMPS
Stand with your legs slightly apart. Jump outwards and stretch your arms out so you look like a star. Then, jump your feet back together and put your arms by your sides.

Do this for 1 minute!

CAT AND COW POSE
Get onto all fours. Push your belly to the floor so your back is arched like a cat.

Then, push your back to the roof so it's rounded like a cow.

Do these poses 5 times each.

HOPPING
Stand on one foot and hop on the spot. Swap your feet and hop on the other foot.

Stretch your arms out to help you balance!

Hop 3 times on each foot!

I AM GRATEFUL   I AM GRATEFUL   HEALTHY EATING   HEALTHY EATING   I LOVE READING   I LOVE READING

I AM GRATEFUL   I AM GRATEFUL   HEALTHY EATING   HEALTHY EATING   I LOVE READING   I LOVE READING

I AM GRATEFUL   I AM GRATEFUL   HEALTHY EATING   HEALTHY EATING   I LOVE READING   I LOVE READING

I AM GRATEFUL   I AM GRATEFUL   HEALTHY EATING   HEALTHY EATING   I LOVE READING   I LOVE READING

I AM GRATEFUL   I AM GRATEFUL   HEALTHY EATING   HEALTHY EATING   I LOVE READING   I LOVE READING

I MOVE MY BODY!   I MOVE MY BODY!   I MOVE MY BODY!   I MOVE MY BODY!   I MOVE MY BODY!   Well Done!

I MOVE MY BODY!   I MOVE MY BODY!   I MOVE MY BODY!   I MOVE MY BODY!   I MOVE MY BODY!   Well Done!

Well Done!   Well Done!   Well Done!   Well Done!   Well Done!   Well Done!